IS-368: Including People With Disabilities in Disaster Operations

By

Fema

2/20/2014

Lesson 1: Introduction and Course Overview

Course Welcome

The purpose of this course is to increase awareness and understanding of the need for full inclusion of disaster survivors and FEMA staff who are:

- People with disabilities.
- People with access and functional needs.

This course is designed for all personnel involved in disaster operations at the Joint Field Office (JFO) and in other disaster facilities and activities.

The course provides an overview of disabilities and access and functional needs and explains how disaster staff can apply inclusive practices in their disaster assignments.

Course Objectives

At the end of this course, you should be able to:

- Explain the importance of including people with disabilities and others with access and functional needs in disaster operations at the JFO and field locations.
- Describe how JFO and field staff can support and include people with disabilities and others with access and functional needs in disaster operations.
- Describe principles and FEMA initiatives that provide a foundation for the integration of people with disabilities and others with access and functional needs in disaster operations.
- Describe the history of the treatment of and services for people with disabilities.
- Identify laws that provide the legal foundation for issues related to people with disabilities and others with access and functional needs.
- Describe the function of the Disability Integration Advisor.
- Describe personal actions to support the integration of people with disabilities and others with access and functional needs in the JFO and field disaster operations.

Lesson Overview

This lesson presents an overview of terminology and core principles related to people with disabilities and others with access and functional needs.

Upon completing this lesson, you should be able to:

- Identify the benefits and importance of including people with disabilities and others with access and functional needs in disaster operations.
- Define key terms and definitions associated with people with disabilities and others with access and functional needs.
- Describe the types of assistance people with disabilities and others with access and functional needs may require during and after a disaster.
- Describe principles and FEMA initiatives that provide a foundation for the integration of people with disabilities and others with access and functional needs in disaster operations.

Including People With Disabilities and Others With Access and Functional Needs in Disaster Operations

Disasters are not selective about the communities or the people they impact.

Disaster survivors include people with disabilities and others with access and functional needs who may experience a greater impact from disasters because of disruptions in their support systems and loss of equipment, supplies, transportation, and communication.

Disaster survivors may turn to family, friends, neighbors, community organizations, the private sector, and government organizations when help is needed.

It is estimated that at least 50 percent of people who visit Disaster Recovery Centers may have some type of disability or access and functional need.

Misconceptions about their needs may interfere with or preclude the provision of assistance required. Misconceptions about their capabilities may also prevent their inclusion as valuable resources for achieving effective community disaster recovery.

This course offers training in the inclusion of people with disabilities and others with access and functional needs in disaster operations. The course is directed toward disaster staff in the Joint Field Office (JFO) and field locations.

You will learn about the support systems people with disabilities and access and functional needs use to maintain their health, safety, and independence. You will learn how disasters can disrupt these support systems and the types of assistance that may be required by disaster survivors. You will also learn how to include people with disabilities and those with access and functional needs in addressing the challenges of disaster response and recovery.

Finally, you will learn how to collaborate with other members of the JFO staff and with external partners to work with disability organizations and others who support disaster survivors with disabilities and others with access and functional needs.

After completing this course, you will have an improved understanding of full inclusion and why it is a vital part of successful emergency management as it relates to people with disabilities and others with access and functional needs in disaster operations.

By effectively working for and with people with disabilities and others with access and functional needs, all disaster staff at the Joint Field Office and field locations can enhance disaster operations while serving the Whole Community.

FEMA's Whole Community Approach

FEMA has embraced a Whole Community approach to emergency management.

This means we implement solutions that serve the entire community and leverage the resources that the entire community brings to the table. For example:

- People who need accessible transportation use resources such as accessible vans or buses with wheelchair lift.
- People who are deaf or hard of hearing can identify local resources such as American Sign Language (ASL) interpreters and Computer Assisted Real-Time Transcription (CART) services.
- The disability community leaders must be embedded in all Long Term Recovery efforts.

Whole Community and Inclusion

People with disabilities and others with access and functional needs are part of every community.

Inclusion of all members of the community in preparedness, response, recovery, and mitigation strengthens the overall emergency management program.

Disaster Impact

Disasters can be especially disruptive to people with disabilities and others with access and functional needs. For example:

- People with mobility disabilities may rely on accessible transportation service providers that are unable to operate after a disaster.

- People who are deaf or hard of hearing may be unable to hear warnings and alerts or actionable instructions for taking personal protective measures.
- People with low vision may lose the use of equipment that voices or enlarges text.
- People without vehicles may find their usual transportation options are unavailable.

The Whole Community needs to work together to anticipate and find solutions to these and similar problems.

How This Training Applies to JFO Staff

The Disaster Survivor Assistance Specialist may be the first FEMA representative to become aware of disaster recovery situations relating to the needs of people with disabilities and others with access and functional needs.

The Safety Officer is responsible for making sure DRCs and other facilities are safe for staff and visitors—including people with disabilities and others who have access and functional needs.

The External Affairs Officer needs to ensure that people with disabilities and others with access and functional needs have equal access to disaster response and recovery messages and information.

In short, everyone involved in the disaster operation needs to understand and include physical, programmatic, and effective communication access for this key segment of the Whole Community in their plans and activities.

JFO Leadership Setting the Example

The Federal Coordinating Officer (FCO) and other members of the JFO leadership can serve as role models by actively seeking opportunities to work with people with disabilities and others with access and functional needs, especially those who are disaster survivors.

Learn how one FCO—Nancy Casper from Region IV—describes her approach to ensuring full inclusion in disaster operations at the JFO and field locations.

JFO and field staff need to be careful about making assumptions about people with disabilities and others with access or functional needs, and we all need to be careful about underestimating their capabilities as well. My advice? If unsure about a person's disability accommodation or access and functional need, just ask them. I have found people to be very up front about their needs and very reasonable about their expectations.

What Does "People with Disabilities" Mean?

Under the Americans with Disabilities Act (ADA), a person with a disability is one who:

1. Has a physical or mental impairment that substantially limits one or more of the individual's major life activities;
2. Has a record of such an impairment; or
3. Is regarded as having such an impairment.

Individual With a Disability

An individual with a disability is a person who has a physical or mental impairment that substantially limits one or more major life activities that an average person can perform with little or no difficulty, or has a record of such impairment, or is regarded as having such impairment. The law defines specific terms as follows:

- **Physical impairment:** Includes disorders of the sense organs (talking, hearing, etc.), motor functions, and body systems such as respiratory, cardiovascular, musculoskeletal, reproductive, digestive, genito-urinary, hemic, lymphatic, skin, neurological, and endocrine systems.
- **Mental impairment:** Includes most psychological disorders and disorders such as organic brain syndrome, learning disabilities, and emotional or mental illness. It specifically excludes various sexual behavior disorders, compulsive gambling, pyromania, and disorders due to current use of illegal drugs.
- **Major life activities:** Include, but are not limited to, caring for oneself, performing manual tasks, seeing, hearing, eating, sleeping, walking, standing, lifting, bending, breathing, learning, reading, concentrating, thinking, communicating, and working. Major life activities also include the operation of major bodily functions, such as the immune system and normal cell growth, which covers persons with HIV or cancer.
- **Substantially limits:** The severity and duration of an impairment determines whether it substantially limits a major life activity. Impairment must last for several months and significantly restrict a major life activity, but an impairment that is episodic or in remission is still a disability if it would substantially limit a major life activity when active. Similarly, an impairment is still regarded as a disability even if the individual uses medication, equipment, learned adaptive behaviors, or other mitigating measures to lessen the effects of the impairment.

Types of Disabilities

People with disabilities include those members of the population who have:

Hearing Disabilities

- More than 36 million people have a hearing disability. They may be deaf, hard of hearing, or deaf/blind.
- Some do not speak; some use American Sign Language or other sign language; some wear hearing aids and some don't.
- About 10% of the U.S. population does not receive information audibly from the television or radio.
- They may not be able to engage in two-way communication in person or over the telephone without an interpreter or assistive communication device.
- Text and printed material may not always give equal access to information to someone who has a hearing disability.

Vision Disabilities

- More than 10 million people have vision disabilities, including those who are blind, have low vision, or are deaf/blind.
- Some of these 10 million people use service animals; some use white canes; some read Braille; some with low vision can read a document with an 18- or 20-point, bold typeface.
- This means most of these 10 million people cannot see a map on television that shows them evacuation routes away from a fire, flood, or violence.
- This also means that alerts or warnings must be received as audible or tactile information in multiple formats.

Speech Disabilities

- Approximately 2 million people have a speech disability that interferes with two-way communication with another person.
- Some of these people use communication boards; some use Speech-to-Speech relay services; some of them do speak, but with hard-to-understand speech; and some do not or will not speak at all.
- Approximately 500,000 people do not have speech that is understood by others.

Mobility Disabilities

- More than 14 million people have mobility disabilities.
- About 3.3 million people over the age of 14 use a wheelchair and another 10 million have used a cane, crutches, or a walker to get around for 6 months or longer.

- Mobility devices, other durable medical equipment, consumable medical supplies, personal assistance services, and architectural access can make the difference between dependence and independence.

Cognitive, Intellectual, Developmental, and Mental Health Disabilities

- 16.1 million people have a cognitive, intellectual, or mental health disability.
- They need early and timely, accurate, and accessible information using plain language.
- Individuals with Cognitive, Intellectual or Developmental Disabilities should be treated in an age-appropriate manner.
- They may need information in plain language, using concrete terms.
- People with Cognitive, Intellectual or Developmental Disabilities may need instructions broken down into smaller steps, repeated or written down.
- They need early, accurate and accessible information in plain language.
- About 6.7 million adults have a mental health disability.
- People with mental health disabilities may lose access to services or medication after a disaster.
- The stress of the disaster may adversely affect someone with a mental health disability. Individuals may need new or additional services after a disaster.
- Avoid making assumptions about a person based on a type of disability or diagnosis.

Brain Injuries

- About 5.3 million Americans live with a long-term disability as a result of acquired brain injury (ABI) or traumatic brain injury (TBI).
- The most frequent causes of brain injury in America are falls and motor vehicle crashes.
- According to the Brain Injury Association of America, "Brain injury is not an event or an outcome. It is the start of a misdiagnosed, misunderstood, under-funded neurological disease. Individuals who sustain brain injuries must have timely access to expert trauma care, specialized rehabilitation, lifelong disease management and individualized services and supports in order to live healthy, independent and satisfying lives."
- Some people who have brain injuries may appear disoriented, confused, and frustrated, and may require assistance completing forms, reporting events in sequence, etc.

Health Maintenance Needs

- About 48% of Americans say they are currently taking prescription medication.
- One in three Americans takes prescription drugs to treat a long-term illness or condition.
- About 6% of children younger than 12 use bronchodilators for asthma.

- For those in ages 20 to 59, antidepressants were the most commonly prescribed drug.
- Access to medication, supplies, accommodations, and assistive devices often prevents or minimizes medical emergencies in the midst of disasters.

What Does "Access and Functional Needs" Mean?

Simply put, people with "access and functional needs" includes individuals who need assistance due to any condition (temporary or permanent) that limits their ability to take action. To have access and functional needs does not require that the individual have any kind of diagnosis or specific evaluation.

Many individuals within the whole community will have access and functional needs during an emergency. For example, a need for assistance to get to a safe place.

More About Access and Functional Needs

Individuals having access and functional needs may include, but are not limited to, individuals with disabilities, seniors, and populations having limited English proficiency, limited access to transportation, and/or limited access to financial resources to prepare for, respond to, and recover from the emergency.

Individuals with access and functional needs, including those with or without disabilities, can be accommodated with actions, services, equipment, accommodations, and modifications including physical/architectural, programmatic, and communications modifications.

Some individuals with access and functional needs have legal protections, including, but not limited to, the right to be free from discrimination based on race, color, national origin (including limited English proficiency), sex, familial status, age, disability, and economic status.

What Are Examples of "Access and Functional Needs"?

Individuals with access and functional needs may include individuals who:

- Are from diverse cultures, races, and nations of origin;
- Don't read, have limited English proficiency, or are non-English speaking; and

- Have physical, sensory, behavioral, mental health, intellectual, developmental, and cognitive disabilities.

This includes individuals who live in the community and individuals who live in institutions or facilities, older adults with or without disabilities, children with or without disabilities and their parents, individuals who are economically or transportation disadvantaged, women who are pregnant, individuals who have chronic medical conditions, and those with pharmacological dependency.

C-MIST Framework for Identifying Needs

The "C-MIST" framework is a tool for identifying the functional needs of people with disabilities or who have access and functional needs before, during, and after a disaster. C-MIST—originally developed by June Isaacson Kailes—is the acronym for:

Communication
Maintaining Health
Independence
Safety, Support Services, and Self-Determination; and
Transportation

Physical and programmatic access, auxiliary aids and services, integration, and effective communication are often enough to enable individuals to maintain their health, safety, and independence in an emergency or disaster situation.

C-MIST Framework

Before, during, and after an incident, individuals with access and functional needs can be assisted to maintain their health, safety, and independence utilizing the "C-MIST" framework[1] to identify their needs. C-MIST is the acronym for **C**ommunication, **M**aintaining Health, **I**ndependence, **S**afety, Support Services, and Self-Determination, and **T**ransportation.

Physical and programmatic access, auxiliary aids and services, integration, and effective communication are often enough to enable individuals to maintain their health, safety, and independence in an emergency or disaster situation. When basic access is not enough, individuals with access and functional needs may have additional requirements in one or more of the following functional areas to participate in and benefit from emergency planning, programs, and services.

By planning to meet the access and functional needs of individuals who are protected from discrimination, planning can also address the needs of a wide range of individuals defined as "at-risk individuals"[2] or "vulnerable"[3] in other Federal statutes or planning documents. Therefore, both statutorily and inclusively, Whole Community planning will necessarily encompass assessing and planning for the equal access and functional needs of individuals and communities.

---

[1]C-MIST has been updated from June Isaacson Kailes' model for purposes of this training and other FEMA uses. The definition has moved away from utilization of a model of defining functional needs in medical terms toward a definition that more accurately addresses medical and nonmedical functional needs in the most integrated setting appropriate and to reduce or prevent decompensation and the development of acute medical conditions. Updates include describing potential barriers and strategies to achieve inclusion, integration, and self-determination; maintenance of health, safety, and independence; and prevention of discriminatory practices in emergency programs.

[2]The term "at-risk individuals" includes children, senior citizens, pregnant women, and others as deemed by the Secretary of HHS (The Pandemic and All-Hazards Preparedness Act (PAHPA), 42 § U.S.C. 300hh-16). To ensure inclusive planning, HHS adopted a functional needs definition of at-risk individuals based on the C-MIST Framework and clarified that individuals who may need additional response assistance also include those who have disabilities, live in institutionalized settings, are from diverse cultures, have limited English proficiency or are non-English speaking, the transportation disadvantaged, have chronic medical disorders, and have pharmacological dependency.

[3]The term "vulnerable populations" includes children, prisoners, pregnant women, mentally disabled persons, economically or educationally disadvantaged persons (CFR Title 45, Part 46).

Individuals' Additional Needs in These Functional Areas

Communication:
Often individuals will require auxiliary aids and services or language access services to initiate effective communication and to receive and respond to information utilizing methods that facilitate effective communication. Individuals may not be able to hear verbal announcements or alerts, see directional signs, communicate their circumstances to emergency responders, or understand how to get assistance due to hearing, vision, cognitive, behavioral, mental health, or intellectual disabilities, and/or limited English proficiency. In addition to auxiliary aids and services, the use of plain language benefits most people.[1]

Maintaining Health:
While most individuals with access and functional needs do not have acute medical needs requiring the support of trained medical professionals, many will require assistance to maintain health and minimize preventable medical conditions. Access to equipment, medication, supplies, bathroom facilities, nutrition, hydration, adequate rest, personal assistance, etc. can make the difference between maintaining health and decompensation, requiring medical care. Additionally, keeping individuals with access and functional

needs with their families, neighbors, and others who can provide assistance will reduce the need for first responders and medical professionals at a time of scarce resources.

Minority and low-income communities may have severely limited access to health and medical services. Ensuring these communities' access and functional needs are met is critical.

Additionally, individuals, including those who are generally self-sufficient and those who have adequate support from personal assistants, family, or friends may need assistance with: managing unstable, terminal, or contagious conditions that require observation and ongoing treatment; managing intravenous therapy, tube feeding, and vital signs; receiving dialysis, oxygen, and suction administration; managing wounds; and operating power-dependent equipment to sustain life. These individuals may require support of trained medical professionals.

Independence:
For individuals with access and functional needs, providing physical/architectural, programmatic, or communications access will allow them to maintain independence in an environment outside their home. For individuals requiring assistance to maintain independence in their daily activities, this assistance may be unavailable during an emergency or a disaster. Such assistance may include durable medical equipment or other assistive devices (wheelchairs, walkers, scooters, communication devices, transfer equipment, etc.), service animals, and/or personal assistance service providers or caregivers. Supplying needed support to these individuals will enable them to maintain or quickly restore their pre-disaster level of independence.

Safety, Support Services, and Self-Determination:
Before, during, and after an emergency, individuals may lose the support of personal assistant services, family, or friends; may find it difficult to cope in a new environment (particularly if they have autism, dementia, Alzheimer's, behavioral, or mental health conditions such as schizophrenia or intense anxiety) or may have challenges accessing programs and services. If separated from their caregivers, young children may be unable to identify themselves; and when in danger, they may lack the cognitive ability to assess the situation and react appropriately. All adults, including adults with access and functional needs, have the right to self-determine the amount, kind, and duration of assistance they require.

Transportation:
Individuals who cannot drive or who do not have a vehicle and individuals who may need assistance in evacuating when roads are blocked or public transportation is not operating may require accessible transportation assistance for successful evacuation. Access to transportation assistance needs to be available to those who rely heavily on public transit, including but not limited to low-income and minority communities. This support may include accessible vehicles (e.g., lift-equipped or vehicles suitable for transporting individuals who use oxygen) or information in alternate formats or other languages about how and where to access mass transportation during an evacuation.

Identifying Common Challenges for People Who Have Access and Functional Needs

While some people with disabilities may need assistance after a disaster, others may be able to maintain their health, safety, and independence without assistance. Ensuring that shelters, recovery centers, messages, and other response and recovery services are accessible for everyone will decrease the likelihood that individuals with disabilities will need additional assistance to maintain their health and independence.

Maintaining Independence

For many individuals, simply providing physical, programmatic, or communications access will allow them to maintain independence in an environment outside their home.

Individuals who require assistance to maintain independence in their daily activities may find this assistance unavailable during an emergency.
Such assistance may include:

- Durable medical equipment or other assistive devices (wheelchairs, walkers, scooters, communication devices, transfer equipment, etc.).
- Service animals and/or personal assistance service providers or caregivers.

Supplying needed support to these individuals will enable them to maintain or quickly restore their pre-disaster level of independence.

Identifying Some Common Access and Functional Needs Challenges

Examples of groups who often have access and functional needs after a disaster are:

- Older adults with disabilities whose communication aids, mobility devices, and other support services are lost or damaged during the disaster.
- Infants and young children who are susceptible to the rapid spread of infectious diseases.
- People with limited English proficiency who may have difficulty communicating their needs.

Examples of People Who Often Have Access and Functional Needs

Older Adults With Disabilities

- More susceptible to health-related problems as a result of the disaster, including hyperthermia or hypothermia.
- May require longer periods of time for recovery from injury or other adverse effects of the disaster.
- May be more susceptible to memory disorders as a result of the disaster.
- May lose or misplace medications during the disaster.
- Communication aids, mobility devices, and other support services may be damaged or lost during the disaster.

Infants/Young Children

- Have important physical, psychological, developmental, and emotional needs that are different from the needs of adults that must be anticipated and addressed in disasters.
- Have ongoing needs that must be addressed by their parents or other caregivers.
- Are highly susceptible in a food or agriculture incident. The amount of food and drink required is proportionately more than for adults.
- Are susceptible to the rapid spread of infectious disease.

Non-English Speaking/Limited English Proficiency

- May have difficulty understanding emergency information as a result of language and literacy barriers.
- May not know who to listen to (i.e., what authorities can be trusted).
- May not understand what kind of help is available from government.
- May be separated from social or family networks.

People Without Vehicles

- May rely on public transportation or help from neighbors, friends, or family members—all of which may not be available due to the disaster.
- May have lost their vehicles as a result of the disaster and so are not aware of other options like public transportation (which may not be available due to the disaster anyway).

Key Principles

FEMA's Office of Disability Integration Coordination (ODIC) utilizes seven Key Principles that guide FEMA's programs and activities related to people with disabilities and others with access and functional needs.

These Key Principles are described in the following section. You will learn more about ODIC and other FEMA initiatives in Lesson 3 of this course.

Key Principle #1: Equal Access

People with disabilities must be able to access the same programs and services as the general population.

Key Principle #2: Physical Access

People with disabilities must be able to access locations where emergency programs and services are provided.

Key Principle #3: Access to Effective Communication

People with disabilities must be given the same information provided to the general population. Communications with people with disabilities must be as effective as communications with others.

Key Principle #4: Inclusion

People with disabilities have the right to participate in and receive the benefits of emergency programs, services, and activities.

Key Principle #5: Integration

Emergency programs, services, and activities typically must be provided in an integrated setting.

Key Principle #6: Program Modifications

People with disabilities must have equal access to programs and services, which may entail modifications.

Key Principle #7: No Charge

People with disabilities may not be charged to cover the costs of measures necessary to ensure equal access and nondiscrimination.

Resources

Select the links below for additional information relating to the content of this lesson.

- Detailed description of FEMA's Whole Community approach to emergency management.
- Americans with Disabilities Act (ADA) Web site.
- Disability etiquette publications.

Lesson Summary

In this lesson, you learned about fundamental terminology and concepts regarding people with disabilities and others with access and functional needs.

In the next lesson, you will learn about highlights of disability history.

Lesson 2: Highlights of Disability History

Lesson Overview

This lesson presents an overview of events that have changed the way American society views people with disabilities and others with access and functional needs. The lesson includes a review of laws designed to protect the rights of people with disabilities.

Upon completing this lesson, you should be able to:

- Describe key events and milestones that influenced changes in American society related to people with disabilities and others with access and functional needs.
- Identify landmark legislation associated with people with disabilities.

Changing Views of Disabilities

As a Nation, we have changed the way we view and interact with people with disabilities and others with access and functional needs. We have also changed and made improvements in policies, programs, and services to assist all people to prepare for and recover from disasters.

Improvements in the design and construction of transportation systems and buildings provide improved physical access. These changes may also improve safety.

Improvements in communication systems and devices help ensure access to information.

Changes in policies and procedures of disaster operations help improve access to programs and information.

Laws have been enacted to protect the rights of people with disabilities and others with access and functional needs. However, this has not always been the case.

These changes have evolved over the past 60 years of American history.

In this lesson, you will learn about early perceptions and treatment of people with disabilities and others with access and functional needs.

You will also learn how major disasters over the past 20 years have drawn attention to the additional impacts on people with disabilities and others with access and functional needs.

Finally, you will learn about the principal laws that help ensure the rights of people with disabilities and others with access and functional needs.

Being aware of disability history helps us understand the importance of providing timely and accessible assistance for all people in disaster operations.

Evolving Perceptions

Views of people with disabilities and others with access and functional needs have evolved over the past 60 years.

Historically, perceptions have affected how these individuals were treated.

Misconceptions

In the past, people with disabilities and others with access and functional needs may have been perceived as:

- Unable to care for themselves.
- Unable to function in daily activities in society.
- Unable to make decisions about medical treatment.

Because of these and other misconceptions, they often were marginalized or excluded from the mainstream of society.

Misconceptions Still Exist

Misconceptions about people with disabilities and others with access and functional needs still exist.

Some of these misconceptions may have an impact on disaster operations. We will now look at some of these misconceptions and their impact on disaster operations.

Misconceptions Versus Reality

The following table shows common misconception. Select the picture next to each misconception to view the reality behind it.

Misconception	Reality
#1: Disaster survivors with disabilities are receiving "extra" services that others don't receive.	Accommodations are meant to allow disaster survivors with disabilities equal access to the same services (and the same level of services) as the general population.
#2: The use of pen and paper is an adequate means of communication for someone who uses sign language.	Pen and paper will not give someone who uses sign language full information. Much communication is lost and this dramatically impacts the individual's decisionmaking.
#3: All people with disabilities who need accommodations have friends and family members who can and should provide those accommodations for them.	Friends and family may not be qualified or appropriate to provide accommodations or they may also be affected by the disaster. Individuals with disabilities have the right to choose the accommodations that work best for them and who they receive assistance from.
#4: Unless we can see the disability, the person does not have a disability.	Many disabilities are not readily apparent, and not all people with disabilities will self-identify.
#5: All people with vision loss use Braille.	With the advent of screen-reader software, braille usage has declined. According to the National Federation of the Blind, in the United States fewer than 10 percent of people who are legally blind read Braille.
#6: All people who are deaf can read English text.	Some people who are deaf use only sign language and are not as comfortable with, or do not use, text.
#7: Only a few people use Braille so it's a waste to go through the effort to provide it.	All FEMA documents need to be available in three alternate formats: of total documents provided, 2% should be Braille, 4% should be large print, and 5% provided in CD/audio or flash drive format.
#8: It is appropriate to make decisions about providing services for people with access and functional needs without their participation in the decisionmaking process.	Nobody knows what a person needs more that the person himself or herself.

#9: If a service is provided to a person with an access and functional need, the same service will be required by another person with the same need.	There is no "one size fits all" situation when it comes to disabilities.
#10: People who are deaf or hard of hearing can always read closed-captioning if they can't hear the radio or a warning siren.	Some people do not read, others do not read well enough to process information requiring immediate action, and unfortunately captioning is still not provided consistently in emergencies.

Marginalization and Exclusion

The marginalization and exclusion of people with disabilities resulting from misconceptions has meant that they are often denied access to facilities and services that benefit the general public.

The impact of this marginalization and exclusion is far-reaching. People with disabilities often:

- Are excluded from certain opportunities for employment.
- Have limited or no access to public buildings and transportation systems.
- Are unable to receive critical safety information over public communication systems.

Outdated Views of Disabilities

In the past, American society has viewed disabilities through the following discredited theories or models:

Moral Model of Disability

The moral model attributes the cause of disabilities to actions that individuals, families, or communities may have taken in their lives. The disability is viewed as a form of "punishment" for those actions.

This view of disability is still prevalent in some cultures today.

Medical Model of Disability

The medical model views disability as a situation caused by disease, accident or trauma, or some other health condition. Since the problem is attributed to a medical condition, the "treatment" involves acute medical care and a cure is the goal.

This model was often applied by placing people with disabilities in institutions while other members of the household went off to work or places where they could be taught skills to help them become "productive and contributing" members of society. This model may also imply that people with disabilities need caring for and have trouble accomplishing many aspects of everyday life in society.

Source: *New Renaissance Magazine,* Renaissance Universal

Current View: Social Model of Disability

The social model views disability as a societal limitation, not an individual problem. Social and physical barriers impede people with disabilities from fully participating or integrating into society.

Since the problem is attributed to social conditions, the solution is to enact social change as a way of ensuring human rights for all members of society.

This model represented a shift to membership in the community and participation in activities of society such as employment, education, recreation, transportation, and housing.

Independence, Self-Sufficiency, and Self-Determination

The 1960s saw a move toward independence, self-sufficiency, and self-determination for people with disabilities and others with access and functional needs.

This development rests on the premise that people with disabilities are best able to judge their own needs and are therefore the most knowledgeable about selecting the best solutions to challenges, barriers, and problems they encounter.

Examples of actions that promote independence, self-sufficiency, and self-determination were presented as the Key Principles in Lesson 1.

The Key Principles

- **Equal Access** - People with disabilities must be able to access the same programs and services as the general population.
- **Physical Access** - People with disabilities must be able to access locations where emergency programs and services are provided.
- **Access to Effective Communication** - People with disabilities must be given the same information provided to the general population.
- **Inclusion** - People with disabilities have the right to participate in and receive the benefits of emergency programs, services, and activities.
- **Integration** - Emergency programs, services, and activities typically must be provided in an integrated setting.
- **Program Modifications** - People with disabilities must have equal access to programs and services, which may entail modifications.
- **No Charge** - People with disabilities may not be charged to cover the costs of measures necessary to ensure equal access and nondiscrimination.

Growth of Support Organizations

Today, many national and local organizations provide support systems for people with disabilities and others with access and functional needs. These organizations vary in services provided and populations served, but typically they provide:

- Advocacy
- Education Programs
- Resources

Organizations That Serve People With Disabilities

Three types of entities that operate in advocacy, protection, support, and/or service-providing roles for people with disabilities are listed below:

- **Government Organizations**, such as local agencies on aging, State protection and advocacy agencies, and county or State departments of health or mental health.
- **Institutional Partners**, such as community healthcare facilities and private accessible transportation providers.
- **Advocacy Groups**, such as local Independent Living Centers, psychiatric survivor peer support groups, and self-advocacy groups of leaders with intellectual disabilities.

Lessons Learned From Recent Disasters (1 of 2)

Disasters often provide valuable insights about strengths and weaknesses in disaster plans.

Recent disasters, such as Hurricane Andrew in 1992, the attacks of September 11th, 2001, and Hurricane Katrina in 2005, revealed shortfalls in plans and preparations for people with disabilities and others with access and functional needs in terms of:

- Notification
- Evacuation
- Emergency transportation
- Sheltering
- Access to medications, refrigeration, and back-up power
- Access to mobility and other assistive devices or service animals while in transit or at shelters, or temporary housing
- Access to information

Many of these "lessons learned" are reflected in new laws or amendments to existing laws pertaining to people with disabilities and others with access and functional needs. Despite this, there have been ongoing physical, programmatic, and effective communication access challenges experienced by people with disabilities and others with access and functional needs in more recent disasters.

There has been significant improvement since the passage of the Post-Katrina Emergency Management Reform Act; however, much more needs to be done to achieve true inclusion.

We will review the applicable laws in the next part of this lesson.

Laws Pertaining to Disability Inclusion and Integration

A number of laws have been enacted to prevent discrimination and protect the rights of people with disabilities and others with access and functional needs, including:

Law	Overview
Fair Housing Act of 1968 and Fair Housing Act as Amended in 1988	The Fair Housing Act of 1968 prohibits housing discrimination on the basis of race, color, religion, sex, disability, familial status, or national origin. The provisions cover all types of housing (regardless of type of funding) intended as a short- or long-term residence, including the following types that are often used to house persons displaced by disasters: • Shelters that house persons temporarily • Transitional housing facilities • Short- and long-term rentals • Manufactured housing
Architectural Barriers Act of 1968	The Architectural Barriers Act requires that facilities designed, built, altered, or leased with funds supplied by the Federal Government be accessible to the public. The law helps ensure that certain federally funded buildings and facilities are designed and constructed to include accessibility for people with disabilities. Facilities constructed prior to the law's enactment generally are not covered, but alterations or leases undertaken after the law took effect are usually included.
Robert T. Stafford Disaster Relief and Emergency Assistance Act (as amended)	The Robert T. Stafford Disaster Relief and Emergency Assistance Act of 1988 (as amended) is the law that authorizes Federal assistance when the President declares a State to be a disaster area. The Stafford Act prohibits discrimination during disaster relief and assistance activities. Section 308 of the Stafford Act was amended by the Post-Katrina Emergency Management Reform Act of 2006 (discussed later) to extend those protections to include race, color, religion, nationality, sex, age, disability, English proficiency, and economic status. The Stafford Act applies to: • FEMA services and operations. • Personnel carrying out Federal assistance functions.

	<ul><li>Other bodies participating in relief operations, including all private relief organizations, contractors, and volunteers.</li></ul>
Rehabilitation Act of 1973	The Rehabilitation Act of 1973 prohibits discrimination against persons with disabilities. Section 504 of the act requires all entities that receive Federal financial assistance to: <ul><li>Effectively communicate with people who have communication disabilities including hearing, vision, or cognitive disabilities.</li><li>Meet accessibility standards in new construction and altered facilities.</li><li>Make changes to policies, practices, procedures, and structures as a reasonable accommodation for individuals with disabilities unless doing so would require a fundamental alteration of the program or constitute an undue financial and administrative burden.</li></ul> Section 504 of the Rehabilitation Act applies to all types of entities that receive Federal financial assistance, regardless of whether they are a governmental agency, a private organization, or a religious entity. It also applies to organizations and entities that receive Federal monies distributed through State or local agencies (subrecipients). Federal financial assistance is defined very broadly. For example, a private nonprofit organization that receives a Federal contract to provide services is covered by Section 504, as is an organization that receives free or subsidized use of Federal property, or is provided staff paid by a Federal agency. Section 508 requires Federal electronic and information technology to be accessible to people with disabilities. An accessible information technology system is one that can be operated in a variety of ways and does not rely on a single sense or ability of the user.
Individuals with Disabilities Education Act (IDEA) of 1975	The Individuals with Disabilities Education Act (IDEA) was enacted in 1968 and has been amended several times to clarify its intent.

| | The law requires that qualifying students be provided a free and appropriate education that prepares them for further education, employment, and independent living.

The law as amended in 2004 also specifies that:

• "Special education and related services should be designed to meet the unique learning needs of eligible children with disabilities, preschool through age 21."
• In order to qualify for IDEA, the student's disability must "result in the student needing additional or different services to participate in school".
• IDEA applies to children affected by disasters, by requiring their return to school along with their peers with the continuation of their Individual Education Plan in place. |
| Americans with Disabilities Act (ADA) of 1990 and ADA Amendments Act of 2008 | The ADA prohibits discrimination on the basis of disability in employment, State and local government, public accommodations, commercial facilities, transportation, and telecommunications. It also applies to the United States Congress.

To be protected by the ADA, one must have a disability or have a relationship or association with an individual with a disability. An individual with a disability is defined by the ADA as a person who has a physical or mental impairment that substantially limits one or more major life activities, a person who has a history or record of such an impairment, or a person who is perceived by others as having such an impairment. The ADA does not specifically name all of the impairments that are covered.

Title II of the Americans With Disabilities Act (ADA) of 1990 requires that State and local governments give people with disabilities an equal opportunity to benefit from all of their programs, services, and activities.

Requirements include meeting specified architectural standards and ensuring effective communication with people who have hearing, vision, or speech disabilities.

Title II also applies to public transportation services, such as city buses and public rail transit (e.g., subways, commuter |

rails, Amtrak). Public transportation authorities may not discriminate against people with disabilities in the provision of their services. They must comply with requirements for accessibility in newly purchased vehicles, make good faith efforts to purchase or lease accessible used buses, remanufacture buses in an accessible manner, and, unless it would result in an undue burden, provide paratransit where they operate fixed-route bus or rail systems. Paratransit is a service where individuals who are unable to use the regular transit system independently (because of a physical or mental impairment) are picked up and dropped off at their destinations.

Title III covers businesses and nonprofit service providers that are public accommodations, privately operated entities offering certain types of courses and examinations, privately operated transportation, and commercial facilities. Public accommodations are private entities who own, lease, lease to, or operate facilities such as restaurants, retail stores, hotels, movie theaters, private schools, convention centers, doctors' offices, homeless shelters, transportation depots, zoos, funeral homes, daycare centers, and recreation facilities including sports stadiums and fitness clubs. Transportation services provided by private entities are also covered by title III.

Public accommodations must comply with basic nondiscrimination requirements that prohibit exclusion, segregation, and unequal treatment. They also must comply with specific requirements related to architectural standards for new and altered buildings; reasonable modifications to policies, practices, and procedures; effective communication with people with hearing, vision, or speech disabilities; and other access requirements. Additionally, public accommodations must remove barriers in existing buildings where it is easy to do so without much difficulty or expense, given the public accommodation's resources.

Title IV addresses telephone and television access for people with hearing and speech disabilities. It requires common carriers (telephone companies) to establish interstate and intrastate telecommunications relay services (TRS) 24 hours a day, 7 days a week. TRS enables callers with hearing and speech disabilities who use TTYs (also known as TDDs) and callers who use voice telephones to communicate with each other through a third-party communications assistant. The Federal Communications Commission (FCC) has set minimum standards for TRS services. Title IV also requires closed captioning of federally funded public service announcements.

The ADA Amendments Act of 2008 broadened the definition of disabilities.

Title IV of the ADA requires that Telecommunications Relay Services (TRS) be made available to individuals with speech and hearing impairments to the fullest extent possible and in the most efficient manner.

Any television public announcement that is produced or funded in whole or in part by the Federal Government must be closed captioned.

Individual With a Disability

An individual with a disability is a person who has a physical or mental impairment that substantially limits one or more major life activities that an average person can perform with little or no difficulty, or has a record of such impairment, or is regarded as having such impairment.

The law defines specific terms as follows:

Physical impairment: Includes disorders of the sense organs (talking, hearing, etc.), motor functions, and body systems such as respiratory, cardiovascular, musculoskeletal, reproductive, digestive, genito-urinary, hemic, lymphatic, skin, neurological, and endocrine systems.

Mental impairment: Includes most psychological disorders and disorders such as organic brain syndrome, learning disabilities, and emotional or mental illness. It specifically excludes various sexual behavior disorders, compulsive gambling, pyromania, and disorders due to current use of illegal drugs.

Major life activities: Include, but are not limited to, caring for oneself, performing manual tasks, seeing, hearing, eating, sleeping, walking, standing, lifting, bending, breathing, learning, reading, concentrating, thinking, communicating, and working. Major life activities also include the operation of major bodily functions, such as the

	immune system and normal cell growth, which covers persons with HIV or cancer. Substantial limits: The severity and duration of an impairment determines whether it substantially limits a major life activity. Impairment must last for several months and significantly restrict a major life activity, but an impairment that is episodic or in remission is still a disability if it would substantially limit a major life activity when active. Similarly, an impairment is still regarded as a disability even if the individual uses medication, equipment, learned adaptive behaviors, or other mitigating measures to lessen the effects of the impairment. The Equal Employment Opportunity Commission (EEOC) has adopted the provisions of the ADA as guiding principles of the Rehabilitation Act.
Telecommunications Act of 1996	The Communications Act of 1934 was amended by the Telecommunications Act of 1996. Among its provisions, the 1996 law required that people with disabilities have access to products and services such as telephones, cell phones, pagers, call-waiting, and operator services that were previously not accessible for many people with disabilities.
Post-Katrina Emergency Management Reform Act of 2006	The Post-Katrina Emergency Management Reform Act of 2006 included provisions that amended the Stafford Act to better integrate consideration of all populations and needs into general emergency management planning, response, recovery, and mitigation. As such, those provisions amended Section 308 of the Stafford Act to extend protection of the rights of all populations, including individuals with disabilities, persons with limited English proficiency, children, and the elderly.
21st Century Communications and Video Accessibility Act of 2010	The 21st Century Communications and Video Accessibility Act requires captioned television programs to be captioned when delivered over the Internet, requires video description on television for people with vision loss, allocates $10 million per year for communications equipment used by people who are deaf-blind, ensures emergency information is accessible to individuals who are blind or have low vision, and provides for accessibility of advanced communications such as text messaging, email, and Web browsing on mobile devices, among several other provisions.

Civil Rights Act	Section 504 of the Rehabilitation Act of 1973, 29 U.S.C. § 794 ("Section 504") prohibits discrimination on the basis of disability by recipients of Federal financial assistance. The Americans with Disabilities Act of 1990, 42 U.S.C. § 12101 et seq. ("ADA"), prohibits discrimination on the basis of disability by both public and private entities, whether or not they receive Federal financial assistance. Providers covered by Section 504 and/or the ADA may not deny benefits or services to qualified individuals with disabilities or provide lesser benefits than they provide to others. In general, an individual with a disability is "qualified" if that person meets the essential eligibility requirements for receipt of services or participation in the program or activity with or without reasonable modification to rules, policies, or practices. The purpose of these laws is to ensure that covered programs are as accessible to persons with disabilities as they are to nondisabled individuals.

Lesson Summary

In this lesson, you learned about events that have changed the way American society views people with disabilities and others with access and functional needs. You also learned about laws associated with people with disabilities and others with access and functional needs.

In the next lesson, you will learn about FEMA inclusive initiatives.

Lesson 3: FEMA Inclusion Initiatives

Lesson Overview

This lesson presents an overview of FEMA initiatives that support inclusion of people with disabilities and others with access and functional needs in disaster operations.

Upon completing this lesson, you should be able to:

- Describe recent programs and guidance supporting the integration of people with disabilities and others with access and functional needs into disaster operations.
- Describe the role and responsibilities of the Office of Disability Integration and Coordination.

Inclusion Steps at FEMA

This lesson provides an overview of FEMA initiatives designed to address lessons learned in past disasters and improve disaster operations for the Whole Community.

FEMA's Accessibility and Accommodation Policies

- FEMA must provide access to Agency programs and activities for people with disabilities equal to the access provided to people who don't have disabilities.
- No qualified individual with a disability shall be denied participation in, or benefit of, any program conducted by FEMA, including employment.
- Explicit references to physical, program, and effective communication access must be included throughout all aspects of disaster operations, including the Incident Action Plan (IAP), the Federal Coordinating Officer's priorities, and in hiring, media relations, messaging, internal and external reporting, and Long-Term Recovery.

The Whole Community

[Stacey Phillips, Live Response Reporter] The Federal Emergency Management Agency is sending a message to the first responder community to modify its current disaster plan to include the whole community because the current plans may unintentionally leave some members of society behind.

August 29, 2005, Benilda Caixeta became a victim of Hurricane Katrina. As a quadriplegic, she made arrangements for a service to come pick her up. But when no one showed, she called emergency responders, family, and friends, but it was too late. All that was left was a stranger on the phone.

[Marcie Roth] There was time during that that it looked like as bad as that hurricane was, that it was passing, and I said to Benilda, it looks like things are going to be okay. The hurricane is passing. You know, people know you are there, and somebody will come and help you very soon. And while we were on the phone, she said to me, the water is rushing in. And then, unfortunately, they found her body and her wheelchair floating several days later.

[Stacey Phillips] Benilda is one of many who have fallen through the cracks of emergency response plans, not through a lack of caring, but through a lack of understanding.

[Craig Fugate] When we run our basic plan documents and frameworks for locals and states to use, it must not have been very good, because every time we had a disaster, we found a group that wasn't being met, so we would add an annex to our plans to talk about the frail elderly, people with disabilities, people that had pets, children, and infants. That's a lot of people not to be in the basic plan.   So fundamentally, I said, something is wrong here. We're not planning for the whole community. We're planning for—we're making the community fit us. I boiled it down and said, look, we have got to quit planning for easy and putting the hard in annexes. Quit planning for easy. Plan for real. Plan for the communities we live in.

[Stacey Phillips] Getting the message heard means hearing from the whole community well before a disaster hits, which is an effort being led by FEMA's Office of Disability Integration and Coordination.

[Marcie Roth] Planning is the key to all of this. When we do an effective job of bringing folks to the table, providing them with the information that they need so that they can be an active participant on the planning team, they are going to be able to bring their resources, their knowledge, their subject matter expertise to the team in the emergency.

Presidential Policy Directive 8, National Preparedness

Another FEMA initiative is Presidential Policy Directive 8 (PPD-8). PPD-8 describes the President's National Preparedness Goal and the Nation's approach to preparing for the threats and hazards that pose the greatest risk.

PPD-8 links the system of preparedness in five mission areas:

1. Prevention

2. Protection
3. Mitigation
4. Response
5. Recovery

PPD-8 supports FEMA's inclusion initiatives by emphasizing the Whole Community approach to preparedness. This means that the Whole Community is to be engaged in all five mission areas.

Because people with disabilities and others with access and functional needs are part of the Whole Community, their engagement in all aspects of the five mission areas is encouraged and supported.

Participation of the Whole Community requires:

- Equal access to preparedness activities and programs without discrimination.
- Meeting the access and functional needs of all individuals.
- Consistent and active engagement and involvement in all aspects of planning.

National Frameworks

Part of the National Preparedness System involves the development of national frameworks.

National frameworks describe critical tasks, coordinating structures, and key roles for developing capabilities within each of the five mission areas.

The National Response Framework stipulates that people with disabilities and others with access and functional needs are to be included in activities and initiatives relating to these mission areas.

The National Recovery Framework states: "The community should provide a forum to engage disaster-impacted individuals, particularly individuals with disabilities, individuals with limited English proficiency, seniors, members of underserved populations, and advocates for children so that their needs and contributions are an integral part of the recovery process and outcome."

Comprehensive Preparedness Guide (CPG) 101

Another FEMA inclusive initiative is CPG 101, Developing and Maintaining Emergency Operations Plans, Version 2.0.

A precept of CPG 101, is "… it is essential to incorporate individuals with disabilities or specific access and functional needs and individuals with limited English proficiency, as well as the groups and organizations that support these individuals, in all aspects of the planning process. When the plan considers and incorporates the views of the individuals and organizations assigned tasks within it, they are more likely to accept and use the plan."

Human Resource Practices

FEMA has adopted human resource practices to hire a more diverse workforce that looks like the communities we serve, including recruiting qualified applicants with disabilities during steady-state and disaster operations.

Involvement of Centers for Independent Living

A Center for Independent Living is a nonresidential private nonprofit agency that is:

- Consumer-controlled
- Community-based
- Cross-disability

Each Center for Independent Living is designed and operated within a local community by individuals with disabilities and provides an array of independent living services.

FEMA has partnered with the National Council on Independent Living to have representatives from Independent Living Centers in Disaster Recovery Centers assist people with disabilities and others with access and functional needs impacted by disasters.

Coordination and Communication With Stakeholders

FEMA brings together disability community leaders, emergency managers, and other key stakeholders to facilitate communication and improve inclusive emergency management practices.

An example is the formation of Long-Term Community Recovery committees during post-disaster recovery operations.

Office of Disability Integration & Coordination

Perhaps the most noticeable FEMA initiative to include people with disabilities and others with access and functional needs was the creation of the Office of Disability Integration & Coordination (ODIC).

The mission of the ODIC is:

To provide guidance, tools, methods, and strategies to integrate and coordinate emergency management inclusive of individuals with access and functional needs.

The ODIC is the central point at FEMA for information, resources, and guidance on issues related to the integration and inclusion of people with disabilities and others with access and functional needs in all aspects of preparedness, response, recovery, and mitigation.

The ODIC Web page provides a wealth of information about activities, initiatives, resources, contacts, and events for FEMA personnel and all interested parties outside the agency.

Disability Integration Specialists and Advisors

FEMA has also hired Disability Integration Specialists for the Regional Offices, and Disability Integration Advisors to work at Joint Field Offices.
Regional Disability Integration Specialists (RDISs) have two primary objectives—to promote fully inclusive practices:

- Throughout all divisions and sections in regional offices and to provide training and technical assistance to all regional staff about disability inclusive practices along with inclusion of people who have access and functional needs.
- In tribal, State, and local jurisdictions throughout their regions. Response is a local community responsibility. RDISs help tribal, State, and local government focus on local resources available to achieve inclusive emergency management and full inclusion within tribal, local, and State government.

The role of the Disability Integration Advisor will be discussed in Lesson 4.

RDIS Video: Increasing Awareness

An important initiative of the Regional Disability Integration Specialists was to develop a video explaining disability tools available at DRCs. The video introduces DRC staff to the types of accessibility equipment and other aids available at DRCs.

Resources

Select the links below for additional information relating to the content of this lesson.

- FEMA's policy on equal rights.
- FEMA Reference Guide on Accommodating Individuals With Disabilities in the Provision of Disaster Mass Care, Housing, & Human Services.
- Presidential Policy Directive 8 (PPD-8).
- CPG 101, Developing and Maintaining Emergency Operations Plans, Version 2.0.
- FEMA Office of Disability Integration & Coordination Web site.
- Ready.gov's information on individuals with access and functional needs.
- FEMA's video tour of Disability Tools in a DRC.

Lesson Summary

In this lesson, you learned about FEMA inclusion initiatives.

In the next lesson, you will learn about the role of the Disability Integration Advisor.

Lesson 4: Role of the Disability Integration Advisor

Lesson Overview

This lesson describes the function of the Disability Integration Advisor in the JFO.

Upon completing this lesson, you should be able to:

- Identify the role of the Disability Integration Advisor.
- Identify the role of the Regional Disability Integration Specialist.
- Distinguish between disability integration, equal rights, and civil rights.
- Distinguish between the functions and responsibilities of the Disability Integration Advisor and Equal Rights Advisor in the JFO.

Role of the Disability Integration Advisor

The Disability Integration Advisor at the JFO engages the disaster-affected community and also advises JFO staff on disability integration issues.

In the community, the Disability Integration Advisor supports a network of local organizations that advocate for and provide services to people with disabilities and others with access and functional needs.

The local network coordinates to resolve problems related to emergency services for disaster survivors such as finding accessible temporary housing, replacing lost and damaged equipment, and arranging transportation. As the community begins to recover, the network promotes disaster preparedness and mitigation among those served.

In the JFO, the Advisor coordinates with a variety of offices and organizations to advise on accessibility and accommodation for disaster survivors and FEMA staff.

For example, the Advisor can assist with site selection for community meeting locations and advise on physical, programmatic, and effective communication accessibility. He or she can assist in arranging sign language interpreters or other accommodations for people who are deaf or hard of hearing.

The Disability Integration Advisor's goal is to work with all JFO staff to find solutions that remove barriers to full participation by people with disabilities and others with access and functional needs.

Disability Integration and Coordination

JFOs and other disaster facilities present ever-changing challenges to full inclusion of people with disabilities and others with access and functional needs.

The Disability Integration Advisor at the JFO receives support from:

- FEMA's national Office of Disability Integration and Coordination, which provides program, policy, and functional coordination for disability integration throughout FEMA, with our Federal partners, and across the country.
- Regional Disability Integration Specialists, who develop, implement, and support regional and State programs and provide support to the Advisors deployed to JFOs in their Regions.

Disability Integration Advisor: Community Role

The Disability Integration Advisor has a role within the community to support the local advocacy and services network.

The Advisor works with local organizations such as Centers for Independent Living that serve people with disabilities.

The Disability Integration Advisor can be the link for:

- Accessible conference call and community meeting capabilities.
- Information about and coordination with FEMA programs.
- DRC accessibility and coordination with disability service providers to help staff DRCs.
- Helping local and statewide NGO disability organizations to understand FEMA and how to partner to meet survivor needs.
- Keeping local and statewide NGO disability organizations advised about relevant disaster information and encouraging broad dissemination to their constituencies.

Examples of Successful Advocacy and Services Networks

Birmingham, AL

Severe tornadoes struck Birmingham in April 2011.

When FEMA arrived, the Birmingham Independent Living Center had already established a working group of about 75 organizations. The Disability Integration Advisor educated the working group about FEMA's role and encouraged local leaders to form a network as the Alabama Interagency Emergency Response Coordinating Committee.

Understanding the community's capabilities and needs, the committee united to locate and communicate information about recovery resources available to individuals. The committee also worked to ensure that individuals with disabilities and others with access and functional needs received important recovery and assistance information.

FEMA provided conference calling capability and conference calls were held daily to provide critical information to individuals with disabilities and chronic illnesses. Additionally, volunteers continuously scanned broadcast media, print, and electronic newspapers to obtain the most accurate information on resources for disaster recovery.

The committee worked together with many organizations, including FEMA, American Red Cross, Alabama's Governor's Office, and numerous others to ensure that all members of the community received information on disaster recovery and assistance available.

The Birmingham network also shared information about preparedness and community programs on mitigation. Those involved were establishing an entity with staying power that outlasted the disaster response. The group is still together, demonstrating community ownership.

Joplin, MO

When a catastrophic tornado hit Joplin in May 2011, the Birmingham Independent Living Center became a mentor for a network forming in Joplin. The Independent Living Center staff arranged meetings, took calls, and arranged captioning for participants who were deaf and hard of hearing.

The Joplin group met with the Birmingham group the first week following the tornado to get advice on starting a similar network. The Joplin group chose to stay local and to involve the American Red Cross and the Missouri emergency management agency. The group held meetings twice a week.

The teamwork was phenomenal and the group was able to help people who needed housing. In the fall, Joplin was able to open schools on time and students with disabilities were able to return at the same time as their peers, which was a rare achievement.

Disability Integration Advisor: JFO Role

The Disability Integration Advisor has an internal role as an advisor to others in the JFO. The Advisor can provide guidance on:

- Disability laws and regulations and FEMA disability policies.
- Helping ensure accommodations for people who need them.
- Equipment and technology options to provide communication accessibility.
- Solutions to disability-related problems.

Roles Within the JFO

JFO Organization	Disability Integration Advisor Role
All	<ul><li>Provide subject-matter expertise as requested.</li><li>Provide guidance on setting up and using FedRelay Captioning and other tools to make conference calls, webinars, and training accessible.</li><li>Advise on Whole Community principles.</li><li>Advise on dissemination of accessible information.</li></ul>
Human Resources	<ul><li>Provide awareness of and contact information for agencies that have employment programs for people with disabilities.</li><li>Provide referral to appropriate FEMA area in the JFO in response to individual requests for employment and related accommodation inquiries.</li></ul>
Environmental and Historic Preservation (EHP)	<ul><li>Advise on interaction between accessibility, environmental protection, and historical preservation.</li><li>Provide subject-matter expertise on environmental and chemical sensitivity.</li></ul>
Comptroller	<ul><li>Provide subject-matter expertise on expenditures of disaster funds for accommodations such as Video Remote Interpreting (VRI) and local hire training and capacity builder advisors to promote full inclusion throughout disaster operations.</li></ul>
Equal Rights Advisor	<ul><li>Collaborate on site selection and modification alternatives for accessibility in JFO and DRC locations.</li><li>Consult on solutions for physical, programmatic, and effective communications access for disaster survivors.</li><li>Coordinate training on disability issues.</li><li>Support inclusive community outreach efforts.</li></ul>
Disaster Field Training Office	<ul><li>Schedule, develop, and deliver disability integration training for JFO staff to supplement this course.</li></ul>

Alternative Dispute Resolution (ADR)	• Provide subject-matter expertise as requested.
Attorney	• Provide subject-matter expertise as requested. Collaborate on policy, regulatory and legal issues.
Contracting and Acquisitions	• Provide subject-matter expertise to contracting officials for acquisition of services and equipment to ensure individuals with disabilities have equal and timely access to disaster information and services.
Logistics	• In coordination with Safety, Security, and the Equal Rights Advisor, provide disability subject-matter expertise to identify, select, activate, and maintain FEMA facilities (Area Field Office, Joint Field Office, Disaster Recovery Centers, etc.). • In coordination with Individual Assistance, provide disability subject-matter expertise to logistics staff on obtaining, operating, maintaining, and storing accessible equipment and services.
Financial Management	• Provide subject-matter expertise on cost-effective strategies for achieving physical access, effective communication access, and programmatic access.
Planning	• Provide subject-matter expertise across all aspects of the planning process to ensure inclusion and integration.
Security	• Provide subject-matter expertise on building access and egress, both routine and emergency. • Provide subject-matter expertise on disability accommodations (service animals, assistive technology, communication, alerts and warnings, evacuation, potential resources and supports for people with disabilities and others with access and functional needs).
Information Technology (IT)	• Provide guidance on achieving 508 compliance. • Advise on using Assistive Technology (AT) to access and integrate with FEMA networks. • Advise on telecommunications access using assistive technology devices and services (Video Relay Service (VRS), Video Remote Interpreting (VRI), CapTel

	phone, TTY, JAWS software, enlarging software, accessibility options on Windows/Windows compatible platforms, speech-text and text-speech software).
Operations	<ul><li>Advise and provide potential solutions to meet obligations in physical, effective communication, and program accessibility throughout the disaster operations.</li><li>Advise of any potential areas of concern and provide alternative solutions if requested.</li><li>Provide guidance on setting up and using FedRelay captioning and other tools to make conference calls, webinars, and training accessible.</li></ul>
Safety	<ul><li>Provide subject-matter expertise on building access and egress, both routine and emergency.</li><li>Provide subject-matter expertise on disability accommodations (service animals, assistive technology, communication, alerts and warnings, evacuation, potential resources and supports for people with disabilities and others with access and functional needs).</li></ul>

Support to the Federal Coordinating Officer (FCO)

The Disability Integration Advisor can:

- Provide the Federal Coordinating Officer (FCO) with advice and potential solutions to meet obligations to provide physical, effective communication, and program accessibility throughout the disaster operation.
- Help the FCO anticipate potential areas of concern and identify alternative solutions to solve problems.

Support to Disaster Survivor Assistance

The Disability Integration Advisor can support Disaster Survivor Assistance with:

- Subject-matter expertise to assist Disaster Survivor Assistance staff with identifying and reporting needs specific to people with disabilities and others with access and functional needs that require action throughout disaster operations.
- Assistance with effective communication between survivors and Disaster Survivor Assistance staff (e.g., assuring that public messaging and information provided at public meetings is accessible).

Support to Individual Assistance

The Disability Integration Advisor can support Individual Assistance with:

- Advice and technical assistance on mass care, feeding, and shelter accessibility.
- Coordination with ESF-6 lead, the American Red Cross, and other entities that provide mass care services.
- Coordination with ESF-8 lead, Health and Human Services.
- Advice and technical assistance on DRC accessibility.
- Advice and technical assistance on applicant services accessibility and immediate needs, issues, and solutions.
- Advice and technical assistance on transportation accessibility throughout disaster operations.
- Voluntary agency coordination to ensure involvement of the accessibility and disability community in Long-Term Recovery Centers, Community Organizations Active in Disaster (COADs), and Voluntary Agencies Active in Disasters (VOADs).
- Subject-matter expertise on housing programs (disaster, temporary, transitional, and permanent housing) and coordination with partner agencies that deal with accessible, affordable community housing in the most integrated setting.
- Information on service delivery within communities, and incorporation of universal design to produce accessible buildings and environments.

Local Organization Resources

Local disability advocacy and service organizations offer:

- Information about service delivery systems within communities.
- Information on disability benefits programs.
- Information on local resources.
- Connections with disability leaders and information about local disability issues, culture, and politics.
- Involvement in Crisis Counseling and information about cultural competencies.
- Involvement in disaster case management.

Support to Long-Term Recovery

The Disability Integration Advisor can support Long-Term Recovery by:

- Facilitating the involvement of disability organizations and community leaders that may have resources, subject-matter expertise, etc.
- Linking disability organizations with the appropriate FEMA programs.
- Providing subject-matter expertise for accessible long-term recovery activities and products.
- Checking for inclusion in State recovery plans and facilitating disability organizations' inclusion in developing and implementing State recovery plans.
- Advising on accessible communication, materials, and content for long-term recovery outreach and educational activities.
- Providing information on service delivery within communities, and incorporation of universal accessibility in design of all buildings and environments.

Support to Mitigation

The Disability Integration Advisor can support Mitigation with:

- Advice and technical assistance on universal accessibility throughout mitigation activities.
- Advice and technical assistance on inclusion of accessibility issues in State Hazard Mitigation Plan.
- Facilitation to involve disability leaders and organizations in mitigation activities.
- Outreach to survivors with disabilities and others with access and functional needs.
- Advice and technical assistance on accessible meetings and communication (materials and content) for mitigation outreach and educational activities, including the National Flood Insurance Program (NFIP).
- Advice on issues related to disparate impact on elevation and other mitigation alternatives.

Support to Public Assistance

The Disability Integration Advisor can support Public Assistance by:

- Advising about accessibility and universal access in construction and restoration projects.
- Providing subject-matter expertise, and facilitating community involvement on accessibility issues.

- Providing subject-matter expertise on the Architectural Barriers Act (ABA), the Uniform Federal Accessibility Standard (UFAS), the Americans with Disabilities Act (ADA), and the Rehabilitation Act.
- Advising about accessible transportation and public transportation routes.
- Advising about return and restoration of communities related to accessibility, such as curb cuts.

Support to External Affairs

The Disability Integration Advisor can support External Affairs with advice and technical assistance about:

- Disability-inclusive messaging for the public, including media partners, governmental partners, the private sector, and Congressional and other stakeholders (including inclusive messaging for use by FEMA senior leadership).
- Accessible public communication in all phases of disaster response, recovery, mitigation, preparedness, and protection.
- Opportunities to portray disability-inclusive practices in products and activities through all stages of a disaster (e.g., still and video images, press releases, media interviews, social media messages, and other products).
- Dissemination of accessible information to community members.
- Meeting accessibility for all public meetings that involve FEMA.
- Understanding how people with disabilities can have equal access to apply for assistance and how to communicate those options to survivors in the community.
- Addition of content inclusive of people with disabilities and others with access and functional needs, such as how to arrange for accessible transportation.
- Availability to act as a spokesperson on disability-inclusive activities underway.
- Guidance on achieving 508 compliance with materials produced.

Assistive Technology (AT)

The Disability Integration Advisor can provide training about equipment and technology options that provide equal access in a DRC, including:

- Accessibility applications via Wi-Fi and cellular connections on 4G iPad 3 devices.
- Video Remote Interpreting (VRI) and Video Relay Service (VRS) capabilities for providing access to effective communication for people who are deaf or hard of hearing.
- Audio and electronic formats.
- Amplified phones and captioned phones.

- Reading magnifiers.
- TTY machine with written printout.
- Materials in Braille or large print.
- Text-to-speech reading software such as Job Access With Speech (JAWS).
- Corresponding symbol signage.

Equal Rights Advisor Relationship

The Disability Integration Advisor is a partner and subject-matter advisor to the Equal Rights Advisor on disability issues.

The Office of Equal Rights:

- Receives and processes all discrimination complaints related to people with disabilities and others with access and functional needs.
- Addresses reasonable accommodation issues for FEMA employees.
- Initiates and monitors solutions for physical, programmatic, and effective communications access in consultation with the Disability Integration Advisor.

Lesson Summary

In this lesson, you learned about the role of the Disability Integration Advisor.

In the next lesson, you will learn about how you can collaborate with others in the JFO to achieve inclusion of people with disabilities and others with access and functional needs.

Lesson 5: Achieving Inclusion Through Collaboration

Lesson Overview

This lesson applies the concepts you learned so far to your work as a member of the disaster operation.

Upon completing this lesson, you should be able to:

- Relate the principles of disability integration to JFO staff activities.
- Identify how JFO staff can support the integration of the access and functional needs of disaster survivors with or without disabilities into disaster operations.
- Identify personal actions to advance the integration of the access and functional needs of disaster survivors with or without disabilities in disaster operations.

Achieving Inclusion

This course emphasizes the importance of achieving inclusion of people with disabilities and others with access and functional needs:

- Lesson 1 introduced the principle of inclusion.
- Lesson 2 provided a brief history of the struggle for full inclusion in society.
- Lesson 3 discussed FEMA inclusion initiatives.
- Lesson 4 addressed the role of the Disability Integration Advisor in helping achieve inclusion.

Inclusion can be achieved in two basic ways:

- Group action and collaboration
- Personal action and commitment

We will now look at these two approaches and discuss how they can be applied to achieve full inclusion by JFO staff.

What Is Collaboration?

Collaboration occurs when organizations or groups produce something by:

- Combining efforts.
- Sharing ownership of the outcome.

- Making joint decisions.
- Exchanging expertise, information, and resources.

Different JFO staff members may collaborate to respond to the needs of a disaster survivor who may have access and functional needs, and to provide equal access to FEMA programs. For example:

- DRC Coordinator/Manager, Logistics Chief, IT staff, Safety Officer, Disability Integration Advisor, and Security Officer perform joint reviews of proposed sites to consider designation of a property for use as a FEMA DRC. Team review assures full accessibility of the site for all disaster survivors and employees.
- The Disaster Survivor Assistance Team (DSAT) identifies survivors in the community with immediate needs to maintain health, safety, and independence.
- External Affairs publicizes a DRC opening using a variety of accessible methods and technology.
- The Safety Officer visits the DRC to check physical accessibility.
- Individual Assistance, Equal Rights, Logistics, and IT staff coordinate with the Disability Integration Advisor to assure needed assistive equipment and resources such as sign language interpreters are in place at the DRC and that training is delivered to all staff.

Collaborate To Respond to the Need

You may recall from Lesson 1 that in a disaster setting, people with disabilities and older adults may:

- Experience health-related problems, including hyperthermia or hypothermia, as a result of the disaster.
- Require longer periods of time for recovery from injury or other adverse effects of the disaster.
- Experience memory disorders as a result of the disaster.
- Lose or misplace medications during the disaster.
- Communication aids, mobility devices, and other support services may be lost or damaged during the disaster.

Collaboration Building Blocks

Successful collaboration is built on a solid foundation that includes a few simple steps:

- Identify the right people to help solve a problem or address an issue;

- Establish a shared purpose or goal (e.g., assist the survivor to meet transportation needs);
- Agree on a plan of action to accomplish the goal (including roles and target deadlines); and
- Implement or follow through to ensure that the action has been taken and the desired outcome has been achieved.
- Review actions taken to identify what worked well and what could be done better next time.

Introduction: Case Study of Collaboration

As you read the following case study, think about how FEMA and the local community might address the current situation.

Three weeks after a devastating tornado struck Joplin, MO, the local Independent Living Center contacted the Disability Integration Advisor about a phone call from a friend of an older couple who were living in the back of a warehouse after losing their home and all of their possessions.

Mrs. A had been using a hospital bed due to paralysis from a stroke 5 years earlier and was being assisted by her husband. When the tornado came through, Mr. A protected his wife by throwing himself on top of her. Both survived with no injuries, but everything they owned was gone.

Through the help of a friend, the couple was living in a two-room area at the back of a warehouse that had a kitchenette, toilet, and a small room they could use as a bedroom. Mrs. A was being assisted by her husband who was legally blind.

The warehouse was located outside of Joplin and there were no transportation services. Every day, Mr. A would hitch a ride to Joplin to pick up supplies he needed for his wife. It was in the upper 90s to low 100s outside.

Mr. and Mrs. A had applied for FEMA assistance but had not yet heard anything.

Case Study of Collaboration

Read as a FEMA Individual Assistance Specialist describes how collaboration allowed the response team to meet the needs of the older couple who lost their home after the Joplin tornado in 2011.

We didn't realize that this couple was living in the back of a warehouse after their home was destroyed. The local Independent Living Center folks alerted the Disability Integration Advisor, and she contacted us. We found out that when the couple registered over the phone, they didn't say they needed accessible housing.

The Disability Integration Advisor assisted the husband to report his current situation and the need for accessible housing.

In response, the couple was immediately placed on the list for accessible housing. In addition, Individual Assistance representatives and the Disability Integration Advisor went to the warehouse where the couple was staying to talk to them about their options.

We learned that the couple had no homeowner's insurance or comprehensive car insurance, and therefore could depend upon only the maximum assistance allowed by FEMA.

The husband initially was hesitant to take housing assistance that he felt others worse off might need, but by the end of the week, the couple was living in accessible temporary housing. The husband reported that their housing was in a quiet part of town backed up against many trees for his wife to look out upon and enjoy.

This assistance was due to the collaboration among Individual Assistance, the DIA, and the Independent Living Center.

Achieving Inclusion Through Personal Action and Commitment

Personal actions and commitment by JFO staff can also help achieve inclusion of people with disabilities and others with access and functional needs in disaster operations.

The principles and practices discussed in this course can provide a foundation for personal action and commitment on the part of JFO staff.

We will now review some of the personal actions that can be taken to help achieve inclusion.

Personal Action #1: Put People First When You Speak

"If thought corrupts language, language can also corrupt thought."
— George Orwell

"People first" language simply means choosing words that are appropriate and respectful by:

- Focusing on people's abilities instead of their limitations.
- Putting the person first to demonstrate his or her dignity and worth.

An example of this approach is to say "people with disabilities" instead of "disabled people."

Language Guidelines for Inclusive Emergency Preparedness, Response, Mitigation, and Recovery

FEMA is committed to working toward emergency management language and practices that are inclusive of people with disabilities, and recognizes the power of language in setting the stage for successful "Whole Community" efforts.

The table below offers language guidelines for referring to people with disabilities and others with access and functional needs. This chart is based on several key principles:

- Use *people-first* language; place the emphasis on the individual instead of the disability.
- Use terms consistent with the integration mandate in the Americans with Disabilities Act, which requires public agencies to provide services "in the most integrated setting appropriate to the needs of individuals with disabilities."
- Use language that is respectful and straightforward.
- Refer to a person's disability only if it is relevant.
- Avoid terms that lead to exclusion (e.g., "special" is associated with "separate" and "segregated" services).
- Avoid terms that are judgmental, negative, or sensational (e.g., special, brave, courageous, dumb, super-human).
- Avoid making assumptions or generalizations about the level of functioning of an individual based on their diagnosis or disability. Individuals are unique and have diverse abilities and characteristics.

Language influences behavior. Inclusive language is a powerful ingredient for achieving successful outcomes that are beneficial for the whole community.

Preferred	Avoid
People with disabilities	The handicapped, the disabled, the impaired
An individual or person with a disability	Disabled person
She has access and functional needs; the access and functional needs of people	Special needs, vulnerable, he's an AFN, the AFNs,

with disabilities; others who also have access and functional needs	
Deaf, hard of hearing, hearing loss, sensory disability	Deaf and dumb, the deaf, mute, hearing impaired
Accessible communication, effective communication	Special communication
He has a speech disability	He has a speech impairment, speech impediment
He is blind, he has low vision	The blind, sight impaired
She has a mobility disability	She's mobility impaired, physically challenged, crippled, an invalid, lame, differently-abled, bedridden, house-bound, a shut-in
She has… (multiple sclerosis, cancer, etc.)	She suffers from, is afflicted with, is stricken with, is impaired by
He uses a wheelchair, he uses a scooter, he uses a mobility device	Wheelchair bound, confined to a wheelchair, wheelchair person
Assistive devices, assistive technology, durable medical equipment	Handicapped equipment, special devices
Power chair, motorized wheelchair	Electric wheelchair
She sustained a spinal cord injury, she has paralysis, she is a spinal cord injury survivor, has paraplegia, quadriplegia	She's paralyzed, she's a cripple, she's trapped in her body, her body is lifeless, crippled, useless
Prosthesis, prosthetic limb	Fake leg, wooden leg, peg leg
He has cerebral palsy	He's spastic, palsied
He has epilepsy, he has seizures	He has spells, fits
She is a little person, she has dwarfism, he is of short stature	She's a dwarf, she's a midget
She has Down syndrome	She's Downs, a Down's kid, mongoloid, retarded
He has a learning disability	He is learning disabled, slow, slow learner, dumb
A person with an intellectual disability, developmental disability	The mentally retarded, retard, retarded, mental retardation, mentally impaired
A woman with a cognitive disability, a person with dementia or Alzheimer's Disease	Senile, demented

A child with a traumatic brain injury or a person who sustained a head injury	Brain damaged, slow
He has autism, he is autistic (this term is preferred by some people with autism)	Mental, mentally impaired, retarded, dumb
She has a mental illness, a mental health disability, psychiatric disability; she has a diagnosis of schizophrenia or bipolar disorder, uses behavioral health services	Emotionally disturbed, disturbed, crazy, psycho, schizo, insane, manic, manic depression, mental, mental patient; she has a behavior problem, she needs behavior management, she's a problem child, she is crazy, she is out of control
Congenital disability, sustained a birth injury, acquired at birth	Birth defect, defective
Children who receive special education services, children with Individual Education Plans	Special education kid, special needs child, rides the short bus, SPED, he's special ed, he is special
Senior, older person, older adult or elder with a disability	The frail elderly, the elderly
Accessible bathroom, accessible parking, accessible housing, accessible transportation	Handicapped bathrooms, handicapped parking, special needs housing, special housing, special transportation
Medical needs, acute medical needs, health care needs	Special medical needs
She requires support or assistance with…	She has a problem with …
Planning with people with disabilities	Planning for the disabled
Whole Community planning, inclusive planning, integrated planning	Special needs planning, special plans, special needs annex
Universal cot, accessible cot	ADA cot, special needs cot, special medical cot
Personal assistance services; personal care assistance for children, youth, and adults; caregiver (more appropriate with children)	Patient care, caregiver (for an adult), carer, takes care of
Functional needs support services in a general population shelter, accessible shelter, universal shelter	Special needs shelter, special shelter, special functional needs shelter
Person who receives disability services	Client, patient (unless referring to the acute care services of a nurse or doctor), burden, welfare case

Disaster survivor	Disaster victim (when used to describe an individual who survived the disaster)

The difference between the right word and the almost right word
is the difference between lightning and a lightning bug.
-Mark Twain

Personal Action #2: Seek Advice

JFO staff will encounter a variety of situations that involve people with disabilities and others with access and functional needs who may be:

- Disaster survivors
- Colleagues at the JFO

Remember that the Disability Integration Advisor is available to answer questions, make appropriate referrals, solve problems, and ensure that there are no barriers to full participation.

Personal Action #3: Show Respect

Practice basic etiquette when meeting people with disabilities and others with access and functional needs.

For example:

- Do not shout at a person who is deaf or hard of hearing unless asked to do so. Speak in a normal tone but make sure your mouth is visible.
- When meeting someone who is blind or has low vision, identify yourself and others with you (e.g., "Jane is on my left and Jack is on my right."). Continue to identify the person with whom you are speaking.
- If the person's speech is difficult to understand, do not hesitate to ask him or her to repeat what was said. Never pretend to understand when you do not.
- Finding a place to sit and talk if a person has decreased physical stamina and endurance, which is preferable to standing during the entire interaction.
- Placing yourself at eye level with the person when conversing. Some ways to accomplish this without drawing attention to yourself are kneeling, sitting on a chair, or standing a little farther away to reduce the steep angle of the sightline. This is effective when interacting with all people who are sitting as well as persons with short stature.

Lesson Summary

In this lesson, you learned about ways to achieve inclusion of people with disabilities and others with access and functional needs into disaster operations.

www.ingramcontent.com/pod-product-compliance
Lightning Source LLC
Chambersburg PA
CBHW081321250726
48662CB00008B/2684